T0151142

THE LITTLE BOOK OF
WILDERNESS

Published in 2022 by OH!
An Imprint of Welbeck Non-Fiction Limited,
part of Welbeck Publishing Group.
Based in London and Sydney.
www.welbeckpublishing.com

Disclaimer:
This book is intended for general informational purposes only and should not be relied upon as recommending or promoting any specific practice, diet or method of treatment. It is not intended to diagnose, advise, treat or prevent any illness or condition and is not a substitute for advice from a professional practitioner of the subject matter contained in this book. You should not use the information in this book as a substitute for medication, nutritional, diet, spiritual or other treatment that is prescribed by your practitioner. The publisher makes no representations or warranties with respect to the accuracy, completeness or currency of the contents of this work, and specifically disclaim, without limitation, any implied warranties of merchantability or fitness for a particular purpose and any injury, illness, damage, death, liability or loss incurred, directly or indirectly from the use or application of any of the contents of this book. Furthermore, the publisher is not affiliated with and does not sponsor or endorse any uses of or beliefs about in any way referred in this book.

ISBN 978-1-80069-189-6

Compiled and written by: Malcolm Croft
Editorial: Lisa Dyer
Project manager: Russell Porter
Design: Tony Seddon
Production: Rachel Burgess

A CIP catalogue record for this book is available from the British Library

Printed in China

10 9 8 7 6 5 4 3 2 1

Illustrations: Freepik.com

THE LITTLE BOOK OF
WILDERNESS

NATURAL INSPIRATION

CONTENTS

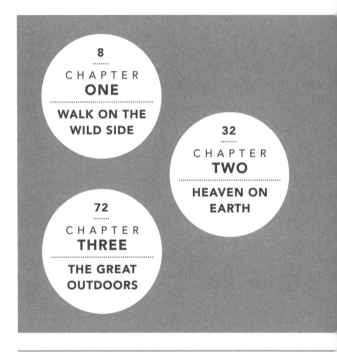

INTRODUCTION

Hello nature-lovers. Welcome to the wilderness.
It's beautiful, isn't it?

Wilderness is as nature intended. The pristine
parts of our perfect planet that still remain wild,
untouched – unscathed – by human hands. From
the sand below to the space above, the seven seas
to an ocean of trees, wilderness comes in all shapes
and sizes, spaces and places, forms and functions.
Wilderness is everywhere. It is in many ways hard to
define precisely, and blindingly apparent: you know
it when you see it. Wilderness is something all your
senses can run wild in. And, yet, paradoxically, it's
also running out. And fast.

In our quest for success and progress, we've
adopted a scorched-earth approach, and many humans
have lost sight of the very thing that defines our
humanity – our harmony with the natural world.
With the raging climate crisis getting worse, and only
slight glimmers of hope, pretty soon there won't be
any wilderness to enjoy. Or, worse, there'll be too
much, but no one left to enjoy it.

Yes, it's time to step back from civilization and get back to nature, gander at the great wide yonder and take a wander in all that is wild; feel your earthly roots at the tip of your toes. And this tiny tome is perfect for wherever you plan to roam.

The Little Book of Wilderness is your back-to-basics, rucksack-friendly companion to help wanderers of all walking speeds reconnect with the wonderful world outside their window. A world that doesn't require Wi-Fi, nor turning off and on again if the buffering buggers up; a place where the only streaming available is the water flow you'll follow.

This bitesize compendium is your hitchhikers' guide to the great outdoors, a celebration of trail blazers, blazing trails and all the other wild stuff that you see when feasting your senses on wilderness. The book is also perfect tinder for a small campfire should you get lost in the woods when your iPhone reception goes feral. We won't mind. Just remember to leave no trace.

So, are you ready to take a walk on our wild side? OK, let's go…

CHAPTER

ONE

Walk on the Wild Side

It's time to pack your bag, pop on your walking boots and open the front door. A whole world of wilderness awaits. Only one question remains: where on earth are we going?

Wild Words #1
Petrichor

One of the most beautiful words in the English language. It describes the scent of rain on dry ground.

Petr- is the Greek root word for "stone", and i*chor* was the word that defined a blood-like substance in the veins of the Greek gods. The word was coined in the 1960s by mineralogists studying the chemical composition of that wonderful nose-tingling scent, so often breathed in on long walks in wilderness.

Know Thy Name #1
Blaze

When wanderlusting in the wilderness, and lost, look to the trees to help you find a path.

A blaze is a coloured marker, usually painted or nailed to a tree. It helps guide hikers when a trail becomes difficult to follow or makes an abrupt turn.

Leave No Trace

The seven principles of enjoying the great outdoors, designed to help backpackers and campers think about ways to minimize the impact that their presence has on the natural environment, are as follows:

1. Plan ahead and prepare

2. Travel and camp on durable surfaces

3. Dispose of waste properly

4. Leave what you find

5. Minimize campfires

6. Respect wildlife

7. Be considerate of other adventurers

Wild Words #2
Mångata

The Swedes know how to put
their language to good use.

Mångata can be translated as
"the path of light that the moon
makes on water". Beautiful.

In July 2020, at the height
of the COVID-19 pandemic,

46 per cent

of people responding to the
People and Nature Survey by
Natural England said they
were spending more time in
nature than ever before.

How to Skip a Stone

No walk on the wild side is complete without skipping a stone at every body of water you find.

According to the Guinness World Records, the most consecutive skips of a stone on water is 88 and was achieved by Kurt Steiner at Red Bridge, near Kane, Pennsylvania, USA, on September 6, 2013. He used a pebble from his 10,000-strong collection of "quality rocks". His perfect pebble weighs 3–8 ounces (85–227g) and is very smooth, flat-bottomed and ¼–⁵⁄₁₆ inch (6–8mm) thick.

More than 40 per cent of people, surveyed by the Office of National Statistics UK, agreed that visiting local green and natural spaces and noticing nature and wildlife was even more important to their health since the COVID-19 lockdown and restrictions began.

Nine out of ten people also agreed that natural spaces are good for mental health and wellbeing.

"

The clearest way
into the Universe
is through a forest
wilderness.

"

John Muir

"

All truly great thoughts are conceived by walking.

"

Friedrich Nietzsche

❝

I wonder if you could
help me. I'm looking for
directions. I'm looking
for the wilderness.

❞

Last of the Summer Wine,
Season 16, Episode 2: "Adopted by a Stray"

Wild Places #1

There are three cities called
Wilderness in America…

Wilderness, Virginia
Wilderness, Missouri
Wilderness, Maryland

Where the Wild Things Are: UK

According to *The Guardian* (2018), these are the top 11 areas of wilderness in the UK.

1. Glen Coe, the Highlands
2. Littondale, Yorkshire Dales
3. Duck's Pool, Dartmoor
4. Mam Nick, Peak District
5. Gwenffrwd–Dinas reserve, Carmarthenshire
6. The Northern Fells, Lake District
7. Mill Bay, Cornwall
8. The Sperrins, Northern Ireland
9. Handa island, north-west Scotland
10. The Rhinogs, Snowdonia
11. Bure Valley, Norfolk

Wild Words #3
Rudènja

From Lithuania, *rudėnja*
describes the way nature begins
to feel as autumn wrestles
control from summer.

Screen Time

Looking for inspiration to get your walking boots on? These ten films set in the great outdoors should get your legs pumping. From deserts to jungles, oceans to forests, they've got your wanderlust covered.

Amundsen (2019)	Rogue (2007)
The Aeronauts (2019)	Apocalypto (2006)
Jungle (2017)	Flight of the Phoenix (2004)
The Lost City of Z (2016)	Forbidden Territory: Stanley's Search for Livingstone (1997)
Kon-Tiki (2012)	
The Ruins (2008)	

66

Dwight will be driving me deep into the Pennsylvania wilderness. …Where he will then leave me to either die or to survive. The choice is yours…This is a very personal, private experience in the wild, that I wish to share it with me, myself and I…When I return, I hope to be a completely changed human being.

99

The Office (US), Season 4, Episode 7: "Survivor Man"

Wilderness in the Wild

Lost in the wilderness in a foreign nation? These translations may help.

Desert – Catalan

Labirint – Albanian

Ødemark – Danish

Divočina – Czech

Erämaa – Finnish

Région sauvage – French

Wildnis – German

Eyðimörk – Icelandic

Wüst – Luxembourgish

Villmark – Norwegian

Pustie – Romanian

Desierto – Spanish

Natura selvaggia – Italian

In 2017, more than 48 million Americans went hiking in wilderness in the US, a 20 per cent increase from 2015.
In 2022, there is expected to be more than

51 million people

who hike regularly, following the conclusion of the COVID-19 pandemic restrictions.

Wandering in the Wilderness #1

The concept of wilderness crops up a lot in the Bible, in particular Moses' 40 years of wandering in the wilderness looking for the Promised Land, as written in the Book of Exodus.

There are many words that have been translated as "wilderness" which occur more than 300 times in the Bible. The most common are Midbar, Arabah and Eremos, often to mean a place of extreme isolation.

Hiking for more than an hour a week can result in up to a **50 per cent** improvement in creative and reasonable thinking and reduces the risk of mental health problems by **50 per cent.**

Be Prepared

Any walk into the wilderness is dangerous,
so plan ahead and take these ten essentials.
They may seem obvious, but more than
350 people a year die in the US when hiking.

1. High-calorie
foods and a large
water canteen

2. Matches/lighter

3. First-aid kit

4. A bivvy sack (for
emergency shelters)
and bin bags

5. Blankets and
cold-weather clothes
(for additional
insulation at night)

6. Water-purifying
tablets

7. Torch/flashlight/
headlight (and
additional batteries)

8. Navigation tools
(e.g. compass, personal
location beacon, maps)

9. Sun protection

10. Multi tool
(Swiss Army knife
or Leatherman)

Wild Words #4
Komorebi

Beams of sunlight filtering down through the trees – that's *komorebi*! When it comes to describing nature, the Japanese language says it best.

Point of Interest #1

If you can't find a stream or lake, suspend and tie a bin bag, or a bivvy sack, above ground to collect rainwater. Be prepared the second you see a cloud.

C H A P T E R

TWO

Heaven on Earth

Wilderness is more than just a place you can go for a nice walk; it's a state of mind. It's a place where you can leave your troubles behind and see the world as Mother Nature intended. If there is a heaven, we'll find it here on Earth. Feel free to follow…

Wild Words #5
Kachou Fuugetsu

Another Japanese word that
describes how the wonder of
beauty and nature can trigger
self-discovery.

Know Thy Name #2
Bluebird Day

Experienced wilderness
warriors use the term Bluebird
Day to describe clear blue
skies – ideal weather for
walks in the woods.

True Wilderness

Looking for a wild spot for your next vacation? According to tripstodiscover.com, these are the 19 last remaining areas of wilderness left on Planet Earth. See them before they turn into holiday resorts.

1. Torngat Mountains National Park, Labrador, Canada

2. Uttarakhand, Himalayas, India

3. Yukon Territory, Canada

4. Westfjords, Iceland

5. Lapland, Sweden

6. Knoydart Peninsula, Scotland

7. Greenland

8. Arctic National Wildlife Refuge, Alaska

9. Olympic National Park, Washington, USA (a million acres of wilderness to explore!)

10. Kakadu National Park,
Northern Territories, Australia

11. Tarkine Rainforest, Tasmania

12. Salar de Uyuni, Bolivia

13. Antarctica

14. Atacama Desert, Chile

15. Great Bear Rainforest,
British Columbia, Canada

16. Bob Marshall Wilderness Complex,
Montana, USA

17. Jarbidge Wilderness, Nevada, USA

18. Golden Trout Wilderness Area,
California, USA

19. Pasayten Wilderness Area,
Washington, USA

Wild Bears

According to the Art of Manliness website (www.artofmanliness.com), this is how you survive a wild bear encounter.

1. Don't run. You can't outrun a bear (top speed: 30 mph). Stand your ground.

2. Hit the ground immediately and curl into the fetal position. Cover the back of your neck with your hands and pray it walks off.

3. Play dead. Bears won't attack if they feel you're no longer a threat (it wastes valuable energy). It may toss you around for a bit, but if you play dead, you'll stay alive.

"

Look deep
into nature,
and then you
will understand
everything
better.

"

Albert Einstein

"

I just wish the world was twice as big and half of it was still unexplored.

"

David Attenborough

Campfire Songs

If you're lost in the woods and you've made a little campfire, sing these songs to stave off any lingering loneliness. Rescue is not far away.

"She'll Be Coming 'Round the Mountain"

"Show Me the Way to Go Home"

"You Are My Sunshine"

"Swing Low, Sweet Chariot"

"Ants Go Marching"

"Ging Gang Goolie"

"The Meatball Song"

"The Quartermaster's Store"

"When the Saints Go Marching In"

"My Bonnie Lies Over the Ocean"

Hiking in nature
for just 20 minutes
can decrease your
body's primary stress
hormone, cortisol,
by approximately
15 per cent.

A Walk in the Woods

Taking a hike in the wilderness? Stay safe with these seven tips, as approved by experts.

1. Tell someone at home where you're going beforehand. And expected time home.

2. Always pack the ten essentials. (see page 29).

3. If you think you're lost, follow the STOP protocol (see page 48).

4. Travel downhill and look for a stream or any body of water.

5. Stay in open areas as much as possible.

6. Try to locate your position or get phone reception.

7. Stay calm and prioritize your health.

Humans can survive
three weeks without
food. But, obviously,
don't try that at home.

Morse Code

If you're lost, find an open
space and spell out HELP in
large branches or clothing.

Failing that, bang loudly on
anything, and use Morse code
as a way of sending an
SOS message.

Point of Interest #2

Take a magnifying glass with
you on any trek into the wild.
Use it to magnify sunlight
on to a leaf or wood shavings
to help start a fire if your
matches get wet. It also doubles
up as a spoon.

Playlist: Get Lost

"Dazed and Confused", Led Zeppelin

"Can't Find My Way Home",
Blind Faith

"Must of Got Lost", J. Geils Band

"We Lost Our Way", Chris Isaak

"Lost", Coldplay

"Forever Lost", Susie Salmon

"Lost in the World", Kanye West
and Bon Iver

"Temporarily Lost", Steven Pasquale

"Lost and Found", Will Smith

"Let's Get Lost", Beck and
Bat for Lashes

STOP

As soon as you admit you're lost, chances are you have been for a while. the best thing to do is Stop, Think, Observe, and Plan. **STOP**.

Stop – Admit you're lost and stop walking.

Think – When did you last see something familiar, a landmark, a trail sign or a person?

Observe – Look around. What can you see that can be helpful to you?

Plan – Devise a strategy that ensures you have water, shelter and heat as quickly as possible.

Wild Foraging

Humans eat only 200 types
of plants*, though scientists
estimate that there are about
100,000 edible species on Earth
– out of the 400,000 different
species of plants.

* Fifty per cent of the plant calories humans consume
come from just three species: rice, wheat and corn.

An average walking pace is approximately 3 mph (4.8 kph). Always keep track of how far you've walked and how long it takes, so you can plot a journey back. Leave blaze markers, or stone markers, called cairns, to ensure you don't walk in circles, if lost.

Wilderness Phobias #1

The wilderness is a frightening place,
and can be full of these things…

1. *Kenophobia* – a fear of wide-open spaces
2. *Achluophobia* – a fear of darkness
3. *Anthophobia* – a fear of flowers
4. *Arachnophobia* – a fear of spiders
5. *Astraphobia* – a fear of thunder
and lightning
6. *Autophobia* – a fear of being alone
7. *Botanophobia* – a fear of plants
8. *Dendrophobia* – a fear of trees
9. *Dystychiphobia* – a fear of accidents
10. *Phobophobia* – a fear of fear

Point of Interest #3

If you're in the northern hemisphere, and you find yourself on your own and in unfamiliar territory, look for moss on trees.

Moss tends to grow on the side of the trees that is not in direct sunlight – north.

(In the southern hemisphere, moss typically grows on the side of the tree that points south.)

Wild Words #6
Hanibaram

A Korean word that can be
translated as "the dry and cool
winds that blow from the west
on a serene day".

Campfire Cocktail:
Campfire Sling

A campfire isn't a campfire until there's a cocktail. Try this one on for size – a Campfire Sling.

Ingredients

2 ounces whiskey
¼ ounce pure maple syrup
3 dashes chocolate bitters
garnish: flamed orange twist

Make It Right

Combine all ingredients in an Old Fashioned glass with a large piece of ice, stir and garnish. All together now, "She'll be coming round the mountain when she comes…"

Going the Distance

If you're going to talk, walk or gawk at wilderness, you better know how far it is to go.

1 Kilometre =	1 Mile =
1,094 yards	1,760 yards
3,281 feet	5,280 feet
1,000 metres	1,609 metres
39,370 inches	63,360 inches
0.621 mile	1.609 kilometres
100,000 cm	160,934 cm

Icons of Wilderness: Greenland

Greenland is effectively one giant ice sheet – 2 miles (3.2 km) deep and 836,330 square miles (over 2 million sq km), or roughly the same as Austria, Belgium, Denmark, France, Germany, Ireland, Italy, Poland, Portugal, the Netherlands and the United Kingdom combined. It's the largest island on Earth, and if all of it melted, worldwide ocean levels would rise 24 feet(7.3 m)!

In Case of Emergency

Recent studies have shown that it takes approximately 120 minutes for a wanderer to feel a natural high from nature, increasing their sense of wellbeing and health – the perfect antidote for our stressful modern lives.

Wild Words #7
Wabi-Sabi

A Japanese word meaning "to find beauty and imperfection and transcience, embracing the natural cycle of birth and decay". Perfect!

10 Most Visited US National Parks (2020)

There are 63 national parks in the U.S., the location where 237 million Americans went to get their dose of wilderness during the COVID-19 pandemic. These are the top ten hotspots to check out.

	Visitors
Great Smoky Mountains	12.1 million
Yellowstone	3.8 million
Zion	3.6 million
Rocky Mountains	3.3 million
Grand Teton	3.3 million
Grand Canyon	2.9 million
Cuyahoga Valley	2.8 million
Acadia	2.7 million
Olympic National Park	2.5 million
Joshua Tree National Park	2.4 million

66

Heaven is under our feet as well as over our heads.

99

Henry David Thoreau

66

We still do
not know one
thousandth of
one per cent of
what nature has
revealed to us.

99

Albert Einstein

America's Most Wild States

The United States is a wild place – but these five states are where most of the wild things are.

Alaska (57,757,130 acres)

California (15,348,149 acres)

Idaho (4,795,700 acres)

Arizona (4,512,066 acres)

Washington (4,484,466 acres)

Wild Words #8
Uitwaaien

A Dutch word where the literal translation is to walk in the wind, or to embark on a walk in nature to clear one's head.

"

Gentlemen, wilderness
weekend is upon us. There
will be no video games,
there will be no internet
pads. This weekend you
have two parents, me
and mother nature.

"

Ron Swanson, *Parks and Recreation*,
Season 4, Episode 4: "Pawnee Rangers"

"
Laws change;
people die; the
land remains.
"

Abraham Lincoln

Wild Words #9
Plimpplampplettere

A Dutch word that means
"to skip stones across water".

66

Wilderness is a spiritual necessity, an antidote to the high pressure of modern life, a means of regaining serenity and equilibrium.

99

Sigurd Olson

Wild Words #10
Utepils

One of our favourite words
– from Norway, naturally –
meaning "to enjoy a beer outside
on a sunny day".

"

There's a whole
world out there,
right outside your
window. You'd be
a fool to miss it.

"

Charlotte Eriksson

66

I go to nature to
be soothed and
healed, and to
have my senses
put in order.

99

John Burroughs

66

Leave the road, take the trails.

99

Pythagoras

CHAPTER
THREE

The Great Outdoors

Out among the wilderness is where the wild things roam. From creatures great and small to trees wide and tall, and everything in between. It's all here: oceans, deserts, space, forests and wide-open lands that run free as far as the eye can see.

Predicting the Weather #1

Knowing what the weather will be when you take a walk on the wild side is important. Heed these handy little ditties…

"Red sky at night, sailors delight.
Red sky morning, sailors take warning."

(A red sky suggests an increase of moisture in the air and that it is likely to rain. If you see a red sky in the morning, a storm is likely to be headed your way!)

Turadh

In Scotland, hikers can enjoy all four seasons in one day, so they say. Apt, then, that there is a Scottish Gaelic term for a break in the clouds between showers.

Know Thy Name #3
Bushwhack

Going off-trail?
That's a bushwhack.

Bushwhacking is the process
of hiking off-piste, often
through dense trees, branches
and bushes. Take something
to whack with you.

Wild Places #2

There are two cities named
Wilderness in South Africa.

Wilderness, Western Cape
Wilderness, KwaZulu-Natal

A three-hour hike
can burn more than
1,200 calories,
if your body weight
is approximately
160 pounds
(11 stone/72.5kg).

A one-hour hike can burn around **450 calories.** Sex, on the other hand, only burns about 70 calories and probably never lasts for an hour.

Point of Interest #4

Foraging for wild food can be a lot of fun, as long as you're certain of what you're eating. If you can't locate berries or nuts, go insect hunting. Some can be nutritious. Just remember, like meat, insects should always be cooked to kill any parasites. Start with these easily locateable snacks.

Ants
Grasshoppers
Maggots
Termites
Earwigs
Beetles

Wild Words #12
Gökota

Another Swedish word of
perfection – *gökota*.
This means "to wake up early
in the morning just to go
into nature to listen to the
first birdsong".

Humans can only survive three days without water. If lost, and in doubt, don't drink your wee.

The fear that strikes upon
first realization of being lost is
hardwired into the human brain.

Millions of years of evolution
have taught humans that being
lost leads to big trouble, and so
the brain becomes scrambled
along with its bearings.

Fight the urge to panic – and
start thinking smart!

Wilderness Phobias #2

Entomophobia – a fear of insects

Heliophobia – a fear of the sun

Hydrophobia – a fear of water

Mysophobia – a fear of dirt and germs

Noctiphobia – a fear of the night

Ombrophobia – a fear of rain

Ornithophobia – a fear of birds

Selenophobia – a fear of the moon

Trypophobia – a fear of holes

Zoophobia – a fear of animals

* Hippopotomonstrosesquipedaliophobia – a fear of long words.
Just in case, you were wondering.

Wild Words #13
Psithurisma

This one's from the Greek language. It means the whispering sound of leaves rustling in the wind. There isn't an English equivalent, sadly.

In 2002, the UK Forestry Commission conducted a survey which found that many people steer clear of forests during hikes and walks due to the feeling they won't be able to find their way out again.

The commission concluded that, "folklore, fairy tales and horror films" have ensured "people are genuinely terrified of getting lost".

"

When you see
someone putting
on his big boots, you
can be pretty sure
that an adventure is
going to happen.

"

A. A. Milne

In 125 CE, Roman Emperor Hadrian went for the first recorded wilderness hike for pleasure in history when he hiked to the summit of Sicily's Mount Etna – to see the sunrise. Mount Etna is one of the most active volcanoes in the world. It would be several centuries before the next hike for pleasure was recorded in the history books.

Wild Words #14
Waldeinsamkeit

Not renowned for their romantic language, German's big contribution to wild words is *waldeinsamkeit* – that feeling of being alone in the woods and connecting with nature. Have you had your *waldeinsamkeit* today?

Wild Words #15
Biophilia

A love of the living world and life; the affinity of human beings for other life forms. This English word describes the connections that humans subconsciously seek with the rest of life on Earth.

66

What we are doing
to the forests of
the world is but a mirror
reflection of what we
are doing to ourselves
and to one another.

99

Mahatma Gandhi

When hiking, never wear cotton socks.*

*Cotton socks soak up sweat and lead to blisters.
Wear wool and synthetic socks.

66

If you truly
love nature, you
will find beauty
everywhere.

99

Laura Ingalls Wilder

William's Wilderness

Shakespeare loved wandering, wondering and writing about wilderness, be it of the mind or the natural world.

These are his most iconic lines. Can you guess the plays they're from?

1. "How quickly nature falls into revolt. When gold becomes her object!"

2. "How hard it is to hide the sparks of nature!"

3. "To hold, as 'twere, the mirror up to nature."

4. "Nature teaches beasts to know their friends."

5. "In nature there's no blemish but the mind. None can be called deformed but the unkind."

6. "One touch of nature makes the whole world kin."

7. "In nature's infinite book of secrecy, a little I can read."

8. "Nature does require her times of preservation."

Henry IV, Part II, Cymbeline, Hamlet, Coriolanus, Twelfth Night, Troilus and Cressida, Antony and Cleopatra, Henry VIII.

However, our favourite
William Shakespeare nature-
related line has to be this,
from *The Merchant of Venice*:

66

I would not have
given it for a wilderness
of monkeys.

99

66

Land really is
the best art.

99

Andy Warhol

"

In all things of nature there is something of the marvellous.

"

Aristotle

66

Wilderness gave us knowledge. Wilderness made us human. We came from here; it is the land of our youth.

99

Boyd Norton

What is Wilderness?

It's quite difficult to precisely define what wilderness is. In 1988, the Finnish Wilderness Committee defined the basic characteristics of wilderness:

1. A wilderness area should comprise a minimum of 37,065 miles (15,000 ha) and usually be more than 6¼ miles (10 km) in width.*

2. The area should be ecologically as diverse as possible and all human action should be adjusted to nature so as not to spoil the wilderness character of the area.

3. The area should as a rule have no roads.

4. The landscape should be in a natural state condition and unspoiled. Any structures connected with human activity should merge with the natural landscape.

*In the USA, the minimum size for an official wilderness area is 4,992 acres (2,020 ha). Australia is 61,776 acres (25,000 ha).

Wild Words #16
Dadirri

An Aboriginal Australian word
to describe understanding the
beauty of nature and being at
peace with yourself.

There are just six states in the US where wilderness is not officially recorded: Connecticut, Delaware, Iowa, Kansas, Maryland and Rhode Island.

Wild Beasts

The word wilderness is derived from the Old English wilddēoren, meaning "wild beasts", and dates back to circa 1200 CE. Before then, the word "deer" (dēor) was used to mean any animal spotted in a forest or on uncultivated land, and so the deer meant beast: the wilderness was anywhere where wild beasts roamed.

One of the first recorded entries of the word was in Sir Gawain and the Green Knight, he of King Arthur legend, and the "Wilderness of the Wirral" story, first written in the 14th century.

66

We are all travellers in
the wilderness of this
world, and the best we
can find in our travels
is an honest friend.

99

Robert Louis Stevenson

"

Walking is a man's
best medicine.

"

Hippocrates

Parks and Recreation

These days, national parks are, for
many, the sole opportunity to wander
among wilderness. They are a great
way to see the great outdoors without
getting too lost. But which nation
has the most?

Australia	**685**	Mexico	**67**
Thailand	**147**	United States	**62**
India	**116**	Colombia	**60**
Brazil	**72**	Indonesia	**54**
Israel	**69**	Russia	**48**

Icons of Wilderness: Yellowstone Park

The world's first national park, Yellowstone, is the sparkliest gem at the heart of America's iconic National Parks. It's big too, weighing in at 3,472 square miles (2.2 million acres), and it's littered with more than 10,000 hydrothermal features such as geysers, hot springs, mud pots and fumaroles. Home to the largest high-elevation lake in North America, the national park also hosts the largest concentration of mammals (67 species) in the whole country, including black and grizzly bears. On average, there is one bear attack per year.

66

Never lose an opportunity of seeing anything beautiful.

99

Ralph Waldo Emerson

66

I could never resist
the call of the trail.

99

Buffalo Bill

35 per cent
of all pharmaceuticals
used in modern
medicine are
molecularly derived
from microorganisms,
plants and animals
found in wilderness.

Wild Words #17
Meriggiare

Trust Italian to nail it beautifully – *meriggiare* – to escape the heat of the midday sun by resting in the shade.

CHAPTER
FOUR

Wide-Open Space

What is wilderness? Can you define something so divine? Like all the best things, wilderness is the stuff of make believe, full of inspiring facts and stats, quotes and notes, that'll make your world spin. Let's dive in…

Know Thy Name #4
GORP

Going for a long walk in the woods?
Remember to pack your GORP.

Granola
Oats
Raisins
Peanuts

A big bag full of salty and savoury foods
that you eat by the handful as a trail mix,
this is a brilliant wilderness snack to fill
you up without weighing you down.

Wild Words #18
Aloha aina

A stunning hint of Hawaiian
to brighten your day – a word
to express one's love of the
natural world.

66

I didn't want some cushy job or a research grant; I wanted 'this' – the farthest reaches of the galaxy, one of the most remote outposts available. This is where the adventure is. This is where heroes are made. Right here – in the wilderness.

99

Star Trek: Deep Space Nine, Season 1,
Episode 1: "Emissary"

Wild Places #3

There is a city
named Wilderness in
Saint Mary, Jamaica.

> **"**
>
> The wilderness, and the idea of wilderness, is one of the permanent homes of the human spirit.
>
> **"**

Joseph Wood Krutch

"

Wilderness is not a luxury but
a necessity of the human spirit,
and as vital to our lives as water
and good bread. A civilization
which destroys what little
remains of the wild, the spare,
the original, is cutting itself off
from its origins and betraying
the principle of civilization itself.

"

Edward Abbey

Point of Interest #5

If you don't know your north from south, and it's starting to get dark, look up…and locate the North Star, or Polaris. If you can see it, you're facing north.

To find the North Star, you'll need to know the Big Dipper constellation.

Put simply, the two outermost stars in the bowl of the Big Dipper point to the North Star.

Food to Pack

When hiking in the great outdoors, avoid snack-idents and pack the right type of food to keep you wanderlusting for as long as you wish.

Peanut butter	Dried fruit
Bananas	Raw vegetables
Beef jerky	Nuts and seeds
Cans of tuna	Protein bars
Granola, oatmeal and porridge	Hard cheeses

"

The wilderness holds answers to questions man has not yet learned to ask.

"

Nancy Newhall

> "
> Speak to the
> earth, and it shall
> teach thee.
> "

Job 12:8

Desert wildernesses occupy approximately **9.5 per cent** of the Earth's total surface and one third (33 per cent) of the land area. Mountainous areas take up about **24 per cent.**

Icon of Wilderness:
Aron Ralston

If you've ever seen the movie 127 Hours, you know the story. On April 26, 2003, experienced American climber Aron Ralston went hiking and rock climbing in Blue John Canyon, Utah. After lowering himself into a canyon, a boulder fell from above and completely trapped his hand. Stuck between a rock and a hard place, Ralston survived for three days on water rationing and drinking his own urine.

On day five, he made the decision to break the bones in his hand to make amputating his own hand easier. Two days later, he had cut off his hand, and was able to free himself and reach safety.

Wilderness Movies

The Great Outdoors (1988)

Wild (2014)

The Way (2010)

The Call of the Wild (1972)

Alone in the Wilderness (2004)

Into the Wild (2007)

A Walk in the Woods (2015)

Captain Fantastic (2016)

The Grey (2011)

127 Hours (2010)

66

The wilderness is infinite in what it offers.

99

Dean Potter

CHAPTER
FIVE

Blazing Trails

From humans to animals, organisms to insects, every single living creature on Earth owes everything it is to the wilderness from which it sprang. Mother Nature created us all. And now she needs you to repay the favour. So, get your boots on, pack the snacks, and take a giant leap into wilderness today.

66

There is no point in
hurrying because you
are not actually going
anywhere. However far
or long you plod, you
are always in the same
place: in the woods.

99

Bill Bryson

"

In wildness is the preservation of the World.

"

Henry David Thoreau

Wild Words #19
Feuillemort

The colour of a faded, dying leaf. Thank you, Français!

66

Now I see the secret of
making the best person.
It is to grow in the open
air and to eat and sleep
with the earth.

99

Walt Whitman

Wilderness
noun

An uncultivated, uninhabited
and inhospitable region.

Predicting the Weather #2

"Circle 'round the moon, rain or snow soon."

(If you look up at the moon and it looks a little hazy, it generally means that rain is up next on the horizon – so maybe delay your trip.)

Wild Words #20
Ammil

A Devon dialect term that describes the thin layer of frost that covers the ground, causing the landscape to glitter like diamonds in the sunlight.

Point of Interest #6

If you add 37 to the number
of chirps a cricket makes in
15 seconds you can determine
the approximate temperature in
degrees Fahrenheit.

Don't Panic!

Always take a whistle with you when you walk in the wilderness. And blow it three times if you suddenly feel lost. Remember, three is the international signal of distress.

So, blow, then wait, turn your body 90 degrees and blow again. Keep doing this.

Spending 20 minutes
in the open air gives
your brain the same
energy boost as a
cup of coffee.

(Better yet, do both
at the same time!)

"

The goal of life is to
make your heartbeat
match the beat of the
universe, to match your
nature with Nature.

"

Joseph Campbell

"

I believe in
God, only I spell
it Nature.

"

Frank Lloyd Wright

Wilderness Act 1964

In 1964, the US government passed a first-of-its-kind Wilderness Act, creating the National Wilderness Preservation System. Today, the Act preserves more than 759 different wilderness areas totalling over 109 million acres of land across 44 states.

The largest wilderness area is located in the Wrangell-Saint Elias Wilderness, Alaska (9 million acres). Only 5 per cent of the US is wilderness – roughly the size of California – with only 2.7 per cent of the nation's total land mass protected wilderness.

Icons of Wilderness:
Patagonia

The last true wilderness, some say, Patagonia is one of the most unspoiled areas on Earth. It contains the Andes mountain range, covers 402,734 square miles (1 million sq km), wild horses run free, and there is roughly one person for every penguin (2 million).

Wild Words #21
Gurfa

An Arabic phrase to describe the amount of water that can be held in one hand.

66

I think nature's imagination is so much greater than man's, she's never going to let us relax.

99

Richard Feynman

66

To sit in the shade on a
fine day and look upon
verdure is the most
perfect refreshment.

99

Jane Austen

"

Life in the woods takes on a neat
simplicity, too. Time ceases to have
any meaning. When it is dark,
you go to bed, and when it is light
again you get up, and everything
in between is just in between. It's
quite wonderful, really.

"

Bill Bryson

Alaska contains approximately half of the wilderness areas in the US.

66

Wilderness is a place where man himself is a visitor who does not remain.

99

US Wilderness Act 1964

Between 1993 and 2009, an area of wilderness the size of 1.27 square miles (3.3 million sq km) – larger than India! – was lost to human activities.

Today, it is estimated
that only 23 per cent
of the Earth's surface
survives as a true
wilderness.

Underwater Wilderness #1

Only 13 per cent of the world's oceans – that is 33.5 million square miles (86.8 million sq km) – have no trace of human life.

And only 5 per cent of the world's oceans are protected.

Wandering in the Wilderness #2

"

Behold, I am doing a new thing; now it springs forth, do you not perceive it? I will make a way in the wilderness and rivers in the desert.

"

Isaiah 43:19

World's Longest Hikes

If golf is a long walk spoiled, wilderness is a long walk somewhere unspoiled. These are the longest hiking trails in the world. If you want to get wild, here's a starter for ten.

1. Great Trail, Canada: 16,780 miles (27,000 km)

2. Great Western Loop, US: 6,875 miles (11,100 km)

3. American Discovery, US: 6,800 miles (10,944 km)

4. Eastern Continental, US: 5,400 miles (8,690 km)

5. North Country, US: 4,598 miles (7,400 km)

6. Great Western, US: 4,455 miles (7,170 km)

7. Sentiero Italia, Italy: 3,832 miles (6,167 km)

8. Continental Divide, US: 3,100 miles (5,000 km)

9. Hokkaido Nature Trail, Japan: 2,849 miles (4,585 km)

10. English Coastal Path, UK: 2,800 miles (4,500 km)

Predicting the Weather #3

*"A rainbow in the morning
is nature's warning."*

(A rainbow means there is
moisture in the air. A rainbow
in the morning means the
moisture is in the western
sky, and a storm could be
headed your way.)

CHAPTER

SIX

Into the Wild

Welcome to the end of the trail. Thanks for coming. But the journey into wilderness is never over. Wilderness is wherever you want it to be. So, what back country will you wander into next?

Wild Words #22
Flâneur

A person who strolls aimlessly
but enjoyably, observing life
and their surroundings.
Are you a *flâneur*?

Short cuts make long delays.

J. R. R. Tolkien, *The Fellowship of the Ring*

According to the UK's Ordnance Survey, one in seven millennials have never read a paper map and would get completely lost without the assistance of a map app on their smart phone device.

A further 53 per cent admitted they would struggle to find their way somewhere without their mobile phone.

At national parks in the US, the daily cost to operate a full-scale search and rescue (SAR) operation is $32,000. Forty per cent of SAR operations are to find lost hikers.

The length of the average search for a lost hiker is 10 hours. Most hikers are found alive.

Forests for the Trees

Forests are a huge part of wilderness and invaluable for oxygen and protecting wildlife.

Today, there are about 3 trillion trees on the planet. Twice as many existed up until 300 years ago, before the start of human civilization.

Ten billion more trees are cut down than are planted every year.

Russia contains the highest volume of forested wilderness on Earth, with more than 800 million hectares.

66

Wildness reminds us what it means to be human, what we are connected to rather than what we are separate from.

99

Terry Tempest Williams

"

It had to do with how it felt to be in the wild. With what it was like to walk for miles with no reason other than to witness the accumulation of trees and meadows, mountains and deserts, streams and rocks, rivers and grasses, sunrises and sunsets.

"

Cheryl Strayed, *Wild: From Lost to Found on the Pacific Crest Trail* (2012)

"

I felt my lungs inflate
with the onrush of
scenery – air, mountains,
trees, people. I thought,
'This is what it is to
be happy.'

"

Sylvia Plath

Wild Words #23
Shinrin-Yoku

A Japanese word that directly
translates as "forest bathing",
a visit to the forest in
order to relax.

September

is National Wilderness
Month in the USA!

Where will you go in
the wild to celebrate?

66

All that is gold
does not glitter,
not all those who
wander are lost.

99

J. R. R. Tolkien, *The Fellowship of the Ring*

Predicting the Weather #4

*"Chimney smoke descends,
our nice weather ends."*

(Set up a campfire. If the smoke from the fire doesn't rise, it indicates a low pressure front moving in. Wet weather is on its way! Be prepared.)

Think desert and you think sand.
But the largest, and driest, place
on Earth is the Antarctic desert
– covering the continent of
Antarctica at around 5.5 million
square miles (14.3 million sq km)
in pure ice and snow.

The term "desert" includes
polar deserts, subtropical deserts,
cold winter deserts and cool
coastal deserts.

In 2020, 53 per cent of Americans (more than 140 million people) of the ages six and over participated in outdoor recreation at least once, the highest participation rate on record.

Can you guess how many points the word "wilderness" is worth in Scrabble?

18 points

The outdoor recreation industry – including wilderness and adventure tourism – generates up to $887 billion annually worldwide.

"

Choose
only one master
— nature.

"

Rembrandt

Wild Words #24
Friluftsliv

When was the last time
you friluftsliv?

Translated from Swedish to
mean "open-air living", it
describes the ancient Nordic
philosophy of aspiring to
live a life outdoors.

66

For most of history,
man has had to fight
nature to survive;
in this century he is
beginning to realize
that, in order to survive,
he must protect it.

99

Jacques-Yves Cousteau

"

Away, away, from men and towns,

To the wild wood and the downs,

To the silent wilderness,

Where the soul need not repress
its music.

"

Percy Bysshe Shelley, *To Jane: The Invitation*

66

The farther one gets
into the wilderness, the
greater is the attraction
of its lonely freedom.

99

Theodore Roosevelt

It is estimated 10 per cent of the world's wilderness – an area the size of the Amazon basin – has been lost since the millennium.

66

Adopt the pace of nature: her secret is patience.

99

Ralph Waldo Emerson

"

Wilderness begins where the road ends; and if the roads never end, there never will be any wilderness.

"

Frank Church

A century ago, around
15 per cent of Earth's surface
was employed by humans
for crops and livestock.

Today, more than 77 per
cent of land – and 87 per
cent of the ocean – has
been modified by human
civilization.

According to the
US Forest Service, an
estimated 6,000 acres
(2,428 ha) of natural,
untouched land and
spaces are modified for
human use *every day*.

"

If adventure has a final and all-embracing motive, it is surely this: we go out because it is our nature to go out, to climb mountains, and to paddle rivers, to fly to the planets and plunge into the depths of the oceans… When man ceases to do these things, he is no longer man.

"

Wilfrid Noyce

"

One thorn of
experience is worth
a whole wilderness
of warning.

"

James Russell Lowell

Americans spend
$524.8 billion on travel
and adventure-related
trips and vacations
every year. Estimates
suggest that hiking will
become the nation's
favourite pastime
by 2040.

In the US, the outdoor recreation industry employs more people every year than finance, construction, education and the oil-and-gas industries combined, about 6 million jobs.

66

Earth and sky, woods and fields, lakes and rivers, the mountain and the sea, are excellent schoolmasters, and teach some of us more that what we could learn from books.

99

John Lubbock

"

Hiking's not for everyone. Notice the wilderness is mostly empty.

"

Sonja Yoerg

Underwater Wilderness #2

The ocean covers
70 per cent of Earth.

80 per cent of it remains
an unexplored wilderness.

But for how long?

66

Without wilderness the world is a cage.

99

David Brower

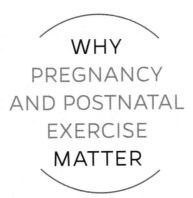

WHY
PREGNANCY
AND POSTNATAL
EXERCISE
MATTER

About the author
Rehana Jawadwala is the founder of MummyYoga, a specialist perinatal yoga service. Since its inception in 2015, she has worked with hundreds of pregnant women and new mothers. She has supported them and their partners in their physical, mental and emotional preparation for birth and parenting.

Rehana has spent over 20 years in the health and fitness industry, in both commercial settings and academia. She writes and speaks extensively on the importance of physical activity during the perinatal period. She has a PhD in exercise physiology and nutrition, and is also an active member of her local Maternity Voices Partnership at the Countess of Chester NHS trust.

Rehana lives in Chester with her daughters, partner and two cats.